Fabian Soci...
No. 503

The Swedish Road To Socialism

Martin Linton

Fabian Tract 503
The Swedish Road To Socialism

CHAPTER

Martin Linton is a political writer on The Guardian where he has written a series of articles about Sweden. He was the Deputy Editor of Labour Weekly from 1971 to 1979.

This pamphlet like all publications of the Fabian Society represents not the collective view of the Society but only the views of the individual who prepared it. The responsibility of the Society is limited to approving the publications it issues as worthy for consideration within the labour movement.

The author would like to thank Björn von Sydow, Alvar Alsterdal, the Fabian readers who read the draft, Krister Walhbäck and Gunilla Nordquist-Turner who read chapters, members of the Fabian Summer School to Sweden in August 1984 whose interest and enthusiasm encouraged him to write the pamphlet and Kathy, Polly and Essie for their patience. It is dedicated to Larry Whitty and all members of the Labour Party.

86 - 7800

320.53
L761s

Cover photo: Sture Ryman

May 1985
ISBN 0 7163 0503 8
ISSN 0307 7523

Typeset by Lithosphere Printing Co-operative Ltd. (T.U.) 01-837 1174
Printed by Blackrose Press (T.U.) 01-251 3043
Published by the Fabian Society, 11 Dartmouth Street, London SW1H 9BN

1. Introduction

Sweden will soon have had a Labour government for 50 years. The Swedish Labour Party and its leader, Olof Palme, are not intending to mark the anniversary and have not even worked out when it falls, as they are too preoccupied with the election that is due this year. But for sympathetic observers, such as the British Labour Party, it may be an appropriate moment at which to pause and consider the reasons for the success of its Swedish sister party and its own relative lack of it.

This pamphlet is not a guide to Swedish politics or even a history of the Swedish Socialdemocratic Labour Party, but a description of the party as it is now and a comparison with its British counterpart, which is intended to shed light on the British Labour Party as much as the Swedish. Chapter 2 looks at the party's ideology and its achievements and Chapter 3 looks at its voting record at elections, where it has maintained a far higher degree of support among its working class voters than the British Labour Party. The explanation that is usually cited before all others is the party's organisation. The Swedish Labour Party has an organisation that puts the Labour Party to shame and is the envy of every party in the Socialist International. That is the subject of Chapter 4. The youth section alone is six times larger than the Labour Party's in spite of a much smaller population. That is the subject of Chapter 5.

But Swedish socialists would be the first to point out that organisation alone cannot win elections and it must be a part of a strategy that starts with political education, consultation, policy formulation, communication and persuasion and only ends with the organisation of elections. If people are looking for the 'secret' of the party's success, they would do better to look at its political education and consultation programmes. They are the subject of Chapter 6.

But political education does not take place in a vacuum and is constantly influenced by the climate of opinion and debate which is influenced in its turn by the press and broadcasting media. This is why the Swedish labour movement sets such a high priority on supporting is own chain of newspapers, the A-press, which is the subject of Chapter 7.

But the labour movement spreads out far more broadly to embrace a family of organisations that have their roots deep in its history, the People's Halls, the People's Parks, the Workers' Educational Association, the Pensioners' Organisation, the National Tenants' Union, the Young Eagles. These are the subject of Chapter 8.

The strongest links in the chain are the trade unions. They have far closer links with the Labour Party than trade unions in Britain and the LO is far closer to the party than its counterpart the TUC. At elections it campaigns openly for a Labour victory and as a result a far higher proportion of trade unionists vote Labour than in Britain. This is the subject of chapter 9.

But the party does not expect to win the votes of trade unionists and give nothing in return. It consults its trade union members through its workplace branches and discovers what reforms they want to see in the party's election manifesto, so that industrial workers feel they have an immediate and tangible interest in a Labour victory.

This is how the Labour Party came to adopt the idea of "wage-earner funds", which came originally from the trade unions and were designed to give workers a share in the ownership of the companies they work for and votes at their annual shareholders' meetings. They are the subject of chapter 10.

But none of these factors can fully explain the success of the Swedish Labour Party and for that we need to go deeper into the party's approach to electoral politics, to the pace of reform, to the shaping of public opinion, to the need to win not just one but successive elections. The real 'secret' of the party's success may well be the party's philosophy of power, which is the subject of Chapter 11.

In conclusion, the Labour Party has a great deal to learn from its Swedish sister party, not by trying to emulate it but by trying to understand the reasons for its success. The Swedish Labour Party, in its early days, drew a great deal of inspiration for the Labour movement in Britain and it is time that the lessons of experience began to flow in both directions.

2. Ideology and Achievements

Sweden is a fascinating country for socialists to study as it has been governed by a socialist party for longer than any other democracy, indeed for longer than almost any other country in the world. Only the Soviet Union can claim to have had a socialist party in power for longer and they have, to put it mildly, a rather different conception of socialism.

Some people in the Labour Party will say, and many more will think, that the Swedish Labour Party is "not really a socialist party, but only social democratic". That is a misunderstanding of the term "socialdemocratic" in its name. It has always meant "socialist and democratic" and was never intended to mean anything else.

It was first used in Germany where Wilhelm Liebknecht and August Bebel founded the Sozialdemokratische Partei Deutschlands (SPD) in 1866. From the start it was a Marxist party. In 1875 it dropped the doctrine of dictatorship of the proletariat in order to merge with Ferdinand Lassalle's General Workers' Union and this angered Marx who disowned the party. But the rest of its programme was still entirely Marxist and it was on this basis that socialdemocratic parties were founded in Denmark (1879), in Norway (1887), in Sweden (1889), in Russia (1898) and in Finland (1899) while the Social Democratic Federation was formed in Britain in 1884, taking its programme from a book by Henry Mayers Hyndman who had plundered and plagiarised Marx without ever acknowledging it. The SDF was one of the organisations that founded the Labour Party in 1900.

The word "socialdemocratic" was coined by Lassalle at a time when the word "socialist" was not yet in wide currency and it referred to exactly those ideas that we would now call "socialist". It is worth noting that in the German language compound adjectives can be formed by dropping the suffix of the first word and subsuming it in the second. Thus "sozialistisch-demokratisch" can be compounded into "sozial-demokratisch". This is not how the word arose but it is how it was understood. Thus the Cassells English-German dictionary gives the German word "sozial-demokratisch" and the English translation "socialist". The Oxford English Dictionary defines a social democrat as "a member of a political party

2

having socialistic views", the word "socialistic" being, in their pedantic view, the correct adjectival form of the noun "socialist".

The difference was originally geographical and historical rather than ideological. The word "socialdemocratic" spread from Germany to north-eastern Europe, so there were Socialdemocratic Parties in Denmark, Sweden, Finland and Russia, where Lenin and Stalin were members of the Russian Social Democratic Party until just before the revolution in 1917 when Lenin changed its name to the Bolshevik Party. In Southern Europe there are Socialist Parties in Austria, Greece, Italy, Spain, Portugal, France and Belgium. In north-western Europe there are Labour Parties in Ireland, Britain, Holland and Norway. In Sweden the traditions overlap in the Socialdemocratic Labour Party, the SAP.

One of these socialdemocratic parties, the West German SPD, decided at its Bad Godesberg conference to remove the more explicit references to state ownership from its party programme and as a result people sometimes use the word "social democratic" to imply a watered down form of socialism. Since then the word has been hijacked by totally non-socialist parties, such as the SDP in Britain and the CDS in Portugal. It is also used by Communists in a quite different sense to refer to all democratic socialist parties that are members of the Socialist International.

But it would be wrong to allow the abuse of the term by the British SDP, influenced by the German SPD, to colour our view of the Swedish party who adopted their name when it had wholly socialist connotations. The Swedish Labour Party is, in fact, every bit as socialist as the British Labour Party, not only in its party programme but in the idealism and the symbolism of the party itself. No one can be in any doubt of this if they have seen a Swedish May Day parade with its sea of red banners or heard how often party members use the word 'socialism' in party debates: "Socialist? Ja visst!" was one of their slogans a few years ago – "Socialist? Yes, of course."

Ideological differences

That is not to say there are no differences in ideology between the British and Swedish Labour parties. There are. The Swedes believe that equality and a high standard of public services are socialist goals that are as important as the common ownership of industry. And in their party programmes, which are revised every 15 years, most recently in 1975, they have shifted the emphasis away from state ownership towards new forms of worker ownership as the alternative to capitalist forms of production, but within the context of an "open" economy with state, co-operative and private sectors.

The British Labour Party has only one subclause of its constitution to define its ideology and this refers to "common ownership of the means of production distribution and exchange" leaving no room, apparently, for a private sector. But what would it say if this were expanded to 25 pages like the programme of the SAP? Readers can judge for themselves whether it would in fact be very different from the SAP's analysis of the past and its aims for the future.

The industrial revolution, says the party programme, brought about an immense rise in production but "periods of rising production alternated with devastating crises that intensified the penury and deprivation of the masses . . . The workers rose against this capitalist system in a struggle for better living conditions, civil rights and a socialist order of society.

"In the teeth of determined resistance from the bastions of established economic and political power, the Swedish working class fought its way to trade union liberties and political democracy . . . Mass poverty and mass unemployment have been eliminated. Inequalities of incomes have been reduced . . . A larger and larger proportion of the results of production has

3

thus been withheld from the distributive principles of capitalism and instead been distributed according to needs . . .

"Despite this the welfare state retains many of the original features of capitalism, such as an unequal distribution of income and wealth . . . Class distinctions still survive . . . In industry, in particular, authoritarian and undemocratic attitudes persist . . Decisions afffecting the entire country are still the prerogative of people guided by considerations of capitalist profit . .

"Internationally capitalism is frequently allied with dictatorship, racial discrimination and oppression. Through the deployment of imperialist power, national liberation movements and progressive democracy are suppressed wherever international capital feels its interests to be in danger . . . Even in countries which have long been ruled by Communist parties, there still remain great differences of income and social status . . . Liberty and equality are stifled . . . The community of free and equal individuals, at which democratic socialism aims, cannot be created in these countries . . . Neither private capitalism nor state capitalism can establish security or justice within nations, nor can they solve the economic and political problems of the world . . .

"The Socialdemocratic Party therefore wishes to replace the present concentration of economic power in private hands by an order of things in which every individual is entitled as a citizen, wage earner and consumer to determine the direction and distribution of production . . . This will be done by involving citizens in the planning of national resources . . . by giving wage earners influence over their firms . . . and a larger share in capital . . . by strengthening the position of consumers . . . In this way the labour movement will continue to struggle for the thoroughgoing transformation of Swedish society, a struggle which began with the democratisation of politics, continued with the establishment of social equality and is now increasingly concerned with the democratisation of the economy."

There has been a clear shift between this party programme, written in 1975, and the earlier 1960 programme. That programme said "the party stands for public ownership or public control of natural resources, banks and industrial and other enterprises so far as it is necessary to safeguard important interests of the community. This qualified commitment to public ownership gives way in the 1975 programme to a belief in the democratisation of the firm as the "main road" by which the party will proceed. A 1984 amendment writes in a commitment to wage-earner funds, a form of worker ownership which the SAP is now introducing.

Priorities

The Swedish Labour Party has always been unenthusiastic about old-style nationalisation. They have a sizable public sector including all the public utilities, public transport, most of the mining, steel and shipbuilding industries, one of the largest banks and a national enterprise board with firms in every sector. But they have never attempted to nationalise the bulk of ordinary manufacturing industry. If that is brought into social ownership, it will be through the state pension fund and the wage-earner funds.

There has always been a stronger emphasis in Swedish socialism on building up the public sector as a whole and not just the public sector of industry. Each successive Labour government has extended the boundaries of the public sector a little further and it is now by far the biggest public sector in the non-Communist world, accounting for 65.4 per cent of Sweden's national income compared with 47 per cent in the UK and 35 per cent in the US. As a corollary it also has the highest overall level of taxation at 59 per cent.

The 'forties and 'fifties and 'sixties were for Sweden decades of unbroken Labour rule during which the welfare state was patiently and laboriously built up. There were few landmarks in this process, except the battle for a universal state occupational pension scheme which the Labour government won after a long parliamentary crisis in 1957, but they were a period of great advances. Visitors can see for themselves what has been achieved if they look at the education system, which is entirely comprehensive, coeducational and with virtually no private sector, or the health service, again with no private sector – the standard is so high that there is little need for it, child care, which is highly developed and allows Sweden to have the highest proportion of working parents, and manpower training on a massive scale which, combined with Keynesian economic policies, keeps their unemployment level below 3 per cent.

The second great priority of Swedish Labour governments has been equality and there has been a constant drive towards the redistribution of wealth and the reduction of wage differentials over the years, so that Sweden now has the greatest degree of equality (or the lowest degree of inequality to be exact) between incomes on almost any definition. It also has the second highest per capita income in the industrialised world, behind Switzerland but ahead of the United States, which flatly disproves all the theories of American economists that their wealth is due to their low taxes or their small public sector and contradicts their claim that only full-blooded capitalism can create wealth. It also goes a long way to explain how Labour stayed in power for so long. It created the wealth and the stability. The bourgeois parties did not.

But in the 'seventies and 'eighties the Swedish Labour Party has had to turn its attention to new sets of problems. Industrial democracy and wage-earner funds are only two of these. The other problems are of an entirely different order. Is there a natural limit to the level of taxation? Has Sweden reached it? Does the welfare state begin, at a certain stage, to conflict with individual liberty? How can Conservative concepts of liberty be challenged by a socialist concept? If the welfare state has reached a maximum level, what happens now? They are intractable quetions that have forced the Labour Party into some fundamental rethinking. There is only one consolation: they are problems of success.

3. Voting Records

What makes Sweden so interesting to study is that it has had nearly 50 years of Labour government under a rigorously democratic system, not by a quirk in the electoral system which allows a party to win with less than 40 per cent of the votes, as in Britain, but under strict proportionality where one can only win a majority of seats with 50 per cent of the votes or something very close to it.

For electoral purposes Sweden is divided into 24 counties and each of them votes on a 'list' system of proportional representation, each party running a list of candidates and a proportion of them elected according to the party's proportion of the vote. There are extra national seats to make sure the final result is precisely proportional. Parties winning less than 4 per cent are excluded.

For the left to win, the SAP (Labour Party) has to win more than 45 per cent of the vote and the VPK (Communist Party) has to come over the 4 per cent threshold. This the left has done in 11 of the last 16 elections. In 1982, for example, the SAP won 45.6 per cent of the vote and the VPK won 5.6 per cent, giving a total of 51.2 per cent and putting the Labour Party in office with the support, or at least the consent, of the VPK.

Coalitions

The opposition is split between the Liberal Party, the Centre Party and the Conservatives, who call themselves the Moderates. In recent years these three non-socialist or bourgeois parties, as they are usually known, have fought elections together on the basis that they will form a coalition government if they win, as they did in 1976 and again in 1979. But there are strong tensions between the three parties which led to the breakup of both coalition governments before the end of their three year parliamentary terms.

It is the SAP that has dominated Swedish politics for the last half century, but this domination must not be overstated. Although the SAP has been in office for 50 years it has not been in power all that time. In the 'twenties the SAP had three brief periods in office but, like the first two Labour governments in Britain in 1924 and 1929, they were minority administrations without real power and dependent on Liberal support, which was not always given.

In 1932 the Labour Party was swept back into office in the middle of an economic crisis and mass unemployment and on a wave of popular support after five trade unionists had been shot dead on a peaceful demonstration at a sawmill in Adalen in northern Sweden. It was to stay there with only one short break for 44 years.

The left had won 50 per cent of the vote for the first time in 1932 but they did not have a majority in the upper house of

parliament and the SAP was able to rule only with an agreement with the Farmers' Party. After a short interregnum in 1936 the SAP returned at the head of a formal coalition with the Farmers' Party and this was broadened into a four-party war-time coalition in 1939. As in Britain, the Labour Party ruled alone for the first time from 1945 to 1951, though it was dependent on the support of the Communists for the last three years.

In 1951 the SAP went back into coalition with the Farmers' Party (now the Centre Party), but from the late fifties until the early seventies the Labour Party had an uninterrupted period of 15 years in power, generally dependent on the support of a handful of Communist MPs exept from 1968 to 1970 when they had an outright majority. In 1973 the election resulted in a tie between left and right and votes in parliament had to be resolved by drawing lots.

It came as something of a shock after the 1976 election for the SAP to find itself out of office. The speaker of the Riksdag still addressed the leader of the SAP as 'Prime Minister' out of habit and former ministers would descend the steps of the parliament building looking in vain for the waiting ministerial car. But to their credit Olof Palme and the Labour Party refused to be numbed by the shock of defeat and fought their way back to a resounding victory in 1982.

So out of nearly 50 years in office the SAP has only been in power on its own for five years, with the support of the Communists for 18, with the Centre Party for 13, in a wartime coalition for six, with the Liberals for five and on a tied vote for three. The idea that the SAP has enjoyed 50 years of hegemony is a myth. It is more realistic to say that the left has been able to rule with a parliamentary majority for 23 years and has had to share power with the right for 23.

When it is calculated in this way the SAP's period in power is longer but not so very much longer than that of the British Labour Party, which has enjoyed an absolute majority in Parliament for 15 years and held office for 20. It is more relevant to bear this comparison in mind – between 23 years and 15 – when comparing the progress made by the two parties towards objectives that are specifically socialist since this kind of progress can only be made with an absolute majority in parliament. On that basis and on almost any definition of socialism the SAP has achieved far more.

Electoral comparisons

But this is to put the comparison at its very lowest level. The SAP has dominated Swedish politics for half a century and has built up a consensus that the non-socialist parties have found it difficult to break. Even when they have been in power bourgeois governments have not been able to reverse most of Labour's economic and social policies. And the SAP has been so dominant because it has been able to – indeed it has had to – build up and maintain a much higher share of the vote than the British Labour Party.

When one looks at the shares of the votes in Swedish elections (Table 1) and in British elections (Table 2), it is clear just how wide the gulf is between the labour movements in the two countries:

* In Sweden the parties of the left have won more than 50 per cent of the vote in ten out of the last 16 elections. In Britain that has never happened.

* In Sweden the Labour Party has won more than 45 per cent of the vote in 11 of the last 16 elections. In Britain the Labour Party has not reached that figure since 1966.

* Even in its worst post-war election result in 1976 the Swedish Labour Party won 42.7 per cent of the vote, which is more than Mrs Thatcher won in her 'landslide' election victory of 1983.

* To win a majority in the Swedish parliament it is necessary to win at least 49 per cent of the vote. In Britain the parties of the left have never once reached this threshold and would never have won power under Sweden's electoral system.

* To put it the other way round the Swedish non-socialist parties have won a majority of votes in only 3 of the last 16 elections, whereas the Conservative and Liberals in Britain have won a majority of the votes in 12 of the last 13 elections, the only exception being 1945 and even in that Labour 'landslide' the combined Conservative and Liberal vote was fractionally ahead of the votes of the left by 48.8 to 48.3 per cent.

It is worth pointing out that the Liberal Party does not play the same role in the two countries. In Britain the Liberals do not form a permanent voting bloc with the Conservatives and many Liberal voters are in fact tactical Labour voters who want to stop a Tory. In Sweden all Liberal voters are clearly voting 'anti-Labour' and the Swedish Liberals are relatively futher to the right, so the British figures are not quite as bad as they seem.

It is also worth pointing out that there has never been a coalition or even a common programme between the SAP and the VPK and their relationship has never been easy, but it is in the nature of Swedish politics that the VPK will never vote to defeat a Labour government on a vote of confidence and put the non-socialist bloc in office. So the election turns on whether the SAP and the VPK will have a combined majority over the non-socialist bloc. So there is a socialist 'bloc' in this important electoral sense as well as in the purely ideological sense that the SAP and VPK are both socialist parties even though their brands of socialism are quite different.

The remarkable fact about the SAP is that is has been able to win so often under a system of PR. The argument against PR has always been that it makes it easier for small parties to thrive but it makes it more difficult for big parties to win majorities. The reason the Labour Party opposes PR is precisely because it fears it would never be able to form a government again unless it was in some kind of alliance with the Liberals.

TABLE 1: percentage shares of the vote in Swedish elections

	Lab	VPK	Socialist bloc	Con	Lib	Centre	Non-socialist bloc
1932	41.7	8.3	50.0	23.1	12.2	14.1	49.4
1936	45.9	7.7	53.6	17.6	12.9	14.3	44.8
1940	53.8	4.2	58.0	18.0	12.0	12.0	42.0
1944	46.6	10.3	56.9	15.9	12.9	13.6	42.4
1948	46.1	6.3	52.4	12.3	22.8	12.4	47.5
1952	46.1	4.3	50.4	14.4	24.4	10.7	49.5
1956	44.6	5.0	49.6	17.1	23.8	9.4	50.3
1958	46.2	3.4	49.6	19.5	18.2	12.7	50.4
1960	47.8	4.5	52.3	16.5	17.5	13.6	47.6
1964	47.3	5.2	52.5	13.7	17.0	13.2	43.9
1968	50.1	3.0	53.1	13.9	15.0	16.5	45.4
1970	45.3	4.8	50.1	11.5	16.2	19.9	47.6
1973	43.6	5.3	48.9	14.3	9.4	25.1	48.8
1976	42.7	4.8	47.5	15.6	11.1	24.1	50.8
1979	43.2	5.6	48.8	20.3	10.6	18.1	49.0
1982	45.6	5.6	51.2	23.6	5.9	15.5	45.0

TABLE 2: percentage shares of the vote in British elections

	Lab	Con	Lib	Con-Lib
1935	37.9	53.7	6.4	60.1
1945	47.8	39.8	9.0	48.8
1950	46.1	43.5	9.1	52.6
1951	48.8	48.0	2.5	50.5
1955	46.4	49.7	2.7	52.4
1959	43.8	49.4	5.9	55.3
1964	44.1	43.4	11.2	54.6
1966	47.9	41.9	8.5	50.4
1970	43.0	46.4	7.5	53.9
1974	37.1	37.9	19.3	56.9
1974	39.2	35.8	18.3	54.1
1979	36.9	43.9	13.8	57.7
1983	27.6	42.4	25.4*	67.8

*Alliance

Under our voting sytem the Labour Party has been able to win a majority in the House of Commons with as little as 39.2 per cent of the vote (in October 1974) whereas the Swedish Labour Party can never win a majority unless the socialist 'bloc' has taken at least 49 per cent of the votes. The threshold of power is much higher.

Ironically, when there was a debate on the elctoral system in Sweden, there was a feeling that the British system was better because of the strong link it creates between electors and elected. But it was a Labour prime minister who turned the idea down in internal party discussions. He thought it was wrong that the Conservatives should have no representation in the "red north" of Sweden. It goes without saying that if Sweden had had the same votes under the British voting system, the SAP would have been in perpetual power with a huge majority over all other parties for 60 years.

As it was, the constitutional reforms that were introduced under a Labour government actually made it more difficult for Labour to retain power. They abolished the upper chamber of Parliament where the Labour Party enjoyed a permanent majority. So the party will have to perform even greater miracles in the future than it has in the past if it wants to enjoy another 50 years in power. But nobody should put it past them.

4. Organisation

Swedish socialists like to present themselves as the country cousins of the Socialist International who may not be very good at theorising about socialism, but can beat everyone else when it comes to putting it into practice. "We probably do not have better ideas or programmes or visions in the Swedish labour movement than in many others," says Arne Geijer, the former leader of the Swedish trade unions, "but we do have an organisation that many others lack. It is with the help of this organisation that we can realise our ideas."

Whether they are right to be so modest about their contribution to socialist theory or whether they are right to be so proud of their socialist achievements so far is open for argument, but there can be no argument about their organisation. It is a superbly effective political machine.

The sheer size of it puts the Labour Party to shame. Sweden has little more than 8 million inhabitants, one seventh of the population of Britain, yet in almost every respect the SAP is bigger than its counterpart in Britain.

Membership

It has a membership of 1,229,703 in 1982 of which some 300,000 were individual members and 900,000 were collectively affiliated through their trade unions.

The Labour Party had about 295,000 individual members in 1983 and about

6,100,000 trade union members. The SAP's individual membership is thus the same as Labour's in absolute terms, but seven times larger in relative terms. Its trade union membership is much smaller in absolute terms but in fact slightly larger in relative terms and it is a very different form of membership.

The Labour Party's trade union 'members' are not members of their constituency Labour Parties at all and pay only 60p a year into party funds, while the SAP's trade union members are full participating and voting members of their local parties and pay something much closer to the full membership rate.

This means that at local level the difference between the parties is enormous. Sundbyberg, a small industrial town in the north-western suburbs of Stockholm, is fairly representative of the SAP. The local party has a membership of 4,417 but that is in a town of only 27,000 inhabitants or about 22,000 electors. That means that about 20 per cent of the voters are Labour Party members, which will seem high by British standards where the average ratio of Labour Party members to electors is 0.7 per cent and the highest (rather incongruously in Waveney, Suffolk) is 3.8 per cent. But 20 per cent is close to the average for Sweden and it has been far higher in Sundbyberg. In 1977 their membership was 7,132.

It must be remembered that the figure includes both individual and trade union members. In an industrial working-class area like Sundbyberg most members are affiliated through their trade union branch (3,583) and only a minority need to affiliate directly to their branches (832). The activists are drawn more equally from both groups but people are not always aware of who is a member through a union and who is an individual member, as it makes no practical difference.

Finances

Of course the SAP at Sundbyberg has the inestimable advantage of receiving state aid of about £72,000 in 1983. This is given at national, county and district level according to the number of MPs or councillors that each party has. The national rate is set by parliament but the local rates vary widely and are highest in the Labour *kommunes*. Sundbyberg gives one of the highest local rates in the country, £1,270 per councillor per year compared with the average of £450. Councillors and MPs also give a fixed proportion of their allowances to the party.

But two points must be borne in mind about state aid. First, they are not the cause of the party's organisational strength, which was there long before state aid began in 1969. The effect of state aid has been mainly to release the party from the need to run bazaars and jumble sales and to relieve the trade unions of the main responsibility for financing the party. It has also ended company donations to the Conservatives, at least publicly.

Before state aid a party like Sundbyberg would have to raise some 60 to 70 per cent of its income from lotteries and fund-raising and 10-15 per cent from membership subscriptions. Now the subscription has dropped in real terms to only £6 a year for individual members, fund-raising is a thing of the past and state aid accounts for a varying proportion of their annual income, 58 per cent in 1981, 49 per cent in 1982, 83 per cent in 1983 and 77 per cent in 1984.

But the other main effect of state aid has been to escalate the organisational and publicity battle between the parties. In relative terms it has not improved the financial position of the SAP and LO but has simply become a necessary part of their income to fight on level terms with the bourgeois parties.

The basic unit of party organisation generally is the *arbetarekommun* which, in its most literal translation, means *workers' commune*. If those words have a rather romantic connation, it is worth pointing out that the word *arbetare* means *worker* but is also used where we use *labour* and *kommun* is the normal word for a district council, so a better translation might be Labour council. It is, in fact, very similar to the Trades and Labour Council that was the predecessor of the modern District Labour Party in many parts of Britain.

Although it is a unit of the Labour Party structure, the *arbetarekommun* acts as a forum for the entire labour movement in a town. It brings together the SAP branches in the area, the affiliated trade union branches, the women's sections, the SSU, the Christian socialists, the workplace branches, in rare cases on a basis of elected delegates as in Britain but more often on the basis that any member may attend. In Sundbyberg, for instance, the *arbetarekommun* has six meetings a year, open to all and attended by 70 members on average. It has two full-time employees, an agent and a secretary.

To be a member of the *arbetarekommun* one can belong to any of its affiliated bodies, so one can join the SSU or the women's organisation directly. One can belong to more than one body – eg trade union branch and local branch – but one must register one's vote in only one place.

At the annual meeting the *arbetarekommun* elects an executive committee and two other committees, the studies and the trade union committees, which tells its own story about the party's priorities. It also elects a banner bearer, a respected position within the party, and delegates to other labour movement organisations and to the party district congress. This congress decides who will go to the party's supreme policy-making body, the triennial congress, whose 350 delegates decide on the party programme, elect the party executive and the party chairman, who is also its leader. The district also decides who goes on the list of election candidates and in what order, so MPs are much more closely tied to and involved in the party.

Electoral strategy

The party is run from its headquarters in Stockholm, which has a relatively small staff and concentrates on the higher realms of election planning and strategy and research. This is a process that never starts because it never stops. As soon as one election is over, the voting research team is busy analysing the results, identifying the party's strong points and weak points, the voter groups that need to be targeted and the areas where resources are needed for the next election in three years' time.

Election planning starts a year and a half before polling day. The strategy has to be ready a year in advance and the manifesto about nine months. At that stage the party district committees come into the picture with local strategies of how they will win the votes of their particular target groups, which might be mothers with pre-school children, pensioners, or white-collar workers. They organise the election meetings and publish the election literature, which usually includes six or seven deliveries per household with full-colour brochures setting out the party's national, regional and local policies, produced by professional volunteers to a very high standard.

From the start of the campaign it is the members of the local *arbetarekommun* who take over the lead. They organise the local meetings, deliveries of leaflets, door-to-door contacts and campaign information booths. Sometimes they are told to locate and talk to very specific groups of votes. Sometimes they react with lightning speed to events in the campaign. A leaflet will be produced overnight to respond to an attack made on the party on television in the evening to be delivered through letter boxes by 6.30am.

Although they make many calls on voters at their homes, they do not canvass in the way that British parties do. They consider it rather 'ungentlemanly' to ask people on the doorstep how they will vote. Nor do they 'knock up' votes on polling day. In fact there is little for party workers to do on polling day. They stand outside the polling station handing out voting lists but they do nothing else. Nor is there any kind of compulsory voting. Yet in Britain, where voters are constantly reminded to vote on polling day and are sometimes almost dragged to the polling booths by overenthusiastic canvassers, the turn out in the last general election was only 72.7 per cent. In Sweden it was 91.4 per cent.

If you ask the SAP how they 'get the vote out', they will tell you that the really important work is not done on polling day, nor even really in the campaign unless it is very close, but a long time ago in the political education of the voters which starts, for most Swedes, in the youth organisations of one or other of the major parties.

5. Youth Organisation

It is in the relative size of their youth organisations that the gap between the parties is greatest. The Labour Party Young Socialists do not publish their membership but internal party surveys have shown that it is about 7,500. On the other hand the membership of the youth section of the Swedish Labour Party, the SSU, is 45,000. That is a ratio of 1:6 in favour of Sweden and when population is taken into account the ratio is 1:42.

The gap is even greater in terms of resources. The Labour Party has only one member of staff working full-time on the LPYS and that is the youth officer. The SSU has 150 full-time agents and about 30 officials.

The Labour Party Young Socialists have one summer school a year and it is held under canvas. The SSU has its own residential school on a three hundred acre site south of Stockholm. It has eight lecture rooms, 20 buildings, accommodation for 110 and it takes 110,000 students during the course of a year, not only from the SSU but from trade unions and other arms of the labour movement.

State aid

It is perfectly true that the SSU has been receiving state aid for a number of years, as have the youth wings of all the political parties since 1959 and indeed the political parties themselves since 1969, but that cannot explain their high membership figures as they were even higher before state aid.

It was in the 'thirties that the SSU became a mass organisation by putting itself at the head of the protest movement against unemployment. Young people flocked to its banner and its membership soared to 104,032 in 1936. In 1937 it bought its residential school and by the late 'fifties, when state aid started, it was already a large organisation employing 30 full-time agents and providing courses for thousands of its members.

State aid was given specifically for recreational activities at first, then for training courses for youth leaders, but during the 'sixties local authorities started to give grants as well and the SSU was able to build up from 30 agents to 150. However, more money has not enabled them to recruit more members. On the contrary, strict rules on the lapsing of members who are no longer active, which the state aid authorities insist on, has meant that the SSU's membership had to be written down from 66,320 in 1982 to 45,000 in 1983. There has also been a long-term trend that has led to a decline in the membership of the youth sections of all the political parties because children are leaving school later and going straight into military service.

As a result the Swedes are not at all proud of the current membership of the SSU. It is not the organisation it once was. But even in its new slimmed-down form it is still by far the largest youth wing of any party in the Socialist International and so much larger than the Labour Party Young Socialists that the comparison is painful. The LPYS would have to have a staff of 1,000 and a membership of a third of a million to be the same size in relation to the population of Britain.

Expulsions

The prospect of a third of a million Young Socialists might give Lord Underhill nightmares in view of the Militant Tendency's iron grip on the LPYS. But if it were to grow to this size, it would very soon become too big for Militant to control. Militant has an interest in keeping it small. So large an LPYS would also be far too important an asset for the party to allow it to be controlled by Militant. The SSU dealt with their own small offshoot of Militant grouped around the newspaper 'Offensiv' in a typically ruthless manner.

It was only when they read about Militant's activities in the Labour Party that they became aware of its links with Offensiv, but they were quick to react. "We thought that mustn't happen so us, so we collected a great deal of information about Trotskyist groups," says the general secretary of the Swedish Labour Party, Bo Toresson.

The SSU decided to take disciplinary action against the supporters of Offensiv as early as 1981, long before the Labour Party expelled the five members of Militant's editorial board in 1983. In Offen-

siv's case there were 150 who were interviewed separately and in the end about 20 recanted and 130 were expelled.

Bo Toresson insists that they were expelled for breaking the rules of the party and not for their Marxist views. Indeed the party can point to its own Marxist roots. "It is always permitted in the SSU to disagree on political questions, but if one openly conducts sectarian activity in an organised form, then it has to be explained that this is incompatible with membership of the SSU. If you look at some of the classic debates in the party, where many people have taken a Marxist position, that has never been grounds for expulsion. It is precisely on the grounds of organised sectarianism that they have been expelled. That's where the boundary goes," he says.

There are some critics of the expulsions in the SAP but they reveal a distinct difference between the two parties' attitudes to their youth sections. The Swedish Labour Party regards the SSU as central to its political strategy, whereas the British Labour Party regards the LPYS as marginal and dispensable. The British Labour Party has expelled the editorial board of Militant but it has left the LPYS under Militant control. This would be unthinkable in the SAP because they regard their youth movement as their chief recruiting agent, their training ground for party and trade union activists, the radical cutting edge that can win the hearts and minds of young people and can push the party in a more radical direction, while the leadership and the elected offices of the SSU – there is no age limit and the age range of the leadership is usually between 25 and 35 – are the nursery slopes for the next generation of party and trade union leaders.

Career structure

Olof Palme was once the international secretary of SSU and Bo Toresson was its national secretary. It is his generation of

SSU leaders who are now taking over many senior positions not only in the SAP, but in the trade unions, the Coop movement, local government and in other branches of the labour movement.

Indeed, this philosophy of picking out talent and grooming it permeates the whole movement. There is only one career ladder which runs through the SSU and the party and into government. Palme was picked out at an early stage and managed to the top without even an election. In more than 95 years the party has had only four leaders. It helps to give the party its aura of permanence.

At the local level the same high priority is given to the work of the SSU. In Sundbyberg, for instance, the party officers regarded it as entirely natural that their executive committee should devote a great deal of time and energy to persuading promising young people to join the SSU.

John Olof Rosander, the leader of the council, was not personally in favour of the expulsion of the three local supporters of Offensiv. He believed it would have been better for young party members to have to argue against supporters of Offensiv and defeat them rather than expel them, just as he had to cut his political teeth on debates with Communists in his union branch, but he was in a minority. Although he is the leading Labour figure in the town, the leader of the council and a member of the party executive, he certainly does not consider a waste of his time to recruit promising youngsters into the SSU. After all, Labour has been in control of the town since 1917 and it has a hand in almost everything that happens in the town, from after school activities for children to tenants' associations and pensioners' clubs and everything in the town that isn't run by the labour movement is run by the Labour council. The new recruits to the SSU are the next generation of party activists, shop stewards, union officials and councillors.

Bo Toresson reflects the same view at national level. "The most important reason for the growth of the SSU is that both the party and the trade unions have given SSU the task of recruiting young people to the party and to the union movement and training them for party and union work. This has been their task and the party has always accepted that the SSU has a great deal of freedom and a great responsibility for the future of the party. That is why the party gives such strong support for the SSU, not only financial support but personal support, and this is where one sees the main difference between the labour and trade union movement in Sweden and in other countries."

6. Political Education

Socialists who come to visit the SAP to seek some kind of explanation of its extraordinary electoral success do not usually feel a need to look any further than the party organisation. A massive membership, an army of full-time agents and state aid for political parties ... they are surely the secret of the SAP's success. But the SAP laughs at the notion that the party's electoral success can be attributed only or even mainly to the efficiency of their electoral machine.

"One can't explain the strength of the party by the number of agents," says the general secretary Bo Toresson. "It's the combination of a strong organisation and attractive policies that counts. Without good policies an organisation can do nothing."

The policies, in their turn, are as good as the people who make them. If it is the ordinary party members who make the party's policies, as it is in the SAP and, in theory at least, in the British Labour Party, then the fate of the party will depend to a great extent on the level of political awareness and understanding and realism of its ordinary members.

The SAP is perhaps the first political party to take this simple lesson to heart and invest as much of its time and energy into the political education of its members and to the process of consulting its members on policy issues as it does to organisation.

In the narrow sense in which the word is usually used in Britain of leafleting and canvassing and getting people out on the day, organisation is merely the final stage in a process that starts with education and consultation and policy formulation and communication and persuasion and only ends with getting voters to the polling station.

To the Swedes it is like plucking the ripe fruit from the tree. What really matters is the choice of the plant, the watering of the soil and the pruning and tending that has been going on all year. They determine whether there is enough fruit on the tree

on harvest day and no amount of extra picking will help if there is not. In the same way no amount of extra canvassers on the night will win an election if the votes are not there.

Self-education

So outside election year the SAP devotes itself to the task of political self-education on a scale that the British Labour Party does not even begin to approach. There are two main methods used: courses, by which they usually mean courses that are residential or away from home, lasting a weekend or a week; and study circles, which usually meet one evening a week and are held in every locality.

The number of members who attend courses varies from 30,000 to 50,000 a year and these can range from general schools for party activists or councillors to special courses on policy issues. The number who attend study circles can vary from 20,000 up to 60,000 in a year and the party has set itself a target of a regular 50,000 participants a year by their centenary year in 1989. The SAP complains that it is still only a minority of its membership that takes part, but to reach the same level the British Labour Party would need to have about 300,000 members attending both courses and study circles, more than its entire individual membership.

At a local level political education is one of the main activities of a local *arbetarekommun*. In Sundbyberg, for example, the annual meeting of the party elects a studies committee to oversee the work on courses, conferences and study circles. In 1983 they sent 93 members on courses for party organisers. They held their own conferences or day schools for branch chairmen, branch organisers, branch treasurers and party representatives on outside bodies. They arranged study circles with a total of 189 participants on every subject from the party programme (34), council social services policy (11), parent-child relations (9), council finances (42), energy conservation (46) and a new housing estate (38). And that does not include members who took part in courses arranged by the party at national or district level.

The study circle is a peculiarly Scandinavian institution, a self-education course based on the idea of group study by five to ten people. It has members, not pupils; meetings, not lessons; and leaders or co-ordinators, not teachers. The idea is that the leader should not lapse into the role of teacher but help the members learn a subject from one another.

Study circles, according to the fanciful theories of educationists, are the pedagogics of the oppressed. But that is hardly surprising since they were pioneered by the labour movement and the free churches at a time when there was no education for the working classes. The main impetus came from Axel Danielsson, one of the founders of the SAP, who said in 1889: "It is clear to every man that the ignorance of the masses ensures that the masses will remain powerless. Well then, fellow proletarians, in this matter there is no other help to be had than self-help. The education of the workers must be accomplished by the workers' own organisations."

The study circle movement has now turned into a national obsession with 1,500,000 participants every year, a quarter of the adult population, many of them taking more than one course. They are not organised by the education authorities, but by voluntary organisations attached to the political parties and the churches, who are refunded for the courses they provide by the state. The biggest and oldest of these is the Workers' Educational Association, the ABF, an arm of the labour movement which caters for about 500,000 participants, a third of the total. Among its main customers are the Labour Party and the trade unions as well as the Communist Party VPK. It is not only concerned with politics, of course, but is the biggest provider of courses in every subject from English to drama and a great educational innovator. It is backed up by the Labour movement's own educational publisher, Brevskolan, which provides all the course material for study circles and is an important part of ABF's success. It had its origins as a working men's correspondence school.

Olof Palme once described Sweden as a "study circle democracy" but it would be more accurate to describe the SAP as a "study circle party". It has a full-time studies agent in each of the 24 district offices and a studies organiser and studies committee in each local party. Even the local branches and clubs are expected to submit their own study circle programmes which the ABF will then organise. They don't need an equivalent to the Fabian Society, they say, because the whole party is a Fabian Society.

Policy making

When it comes to policy making, the SAP has much the same system at the British Labour Party where local parties can submit motions to the district or national congress. But the SAP also has a method of consulting the membership of the party on policy statements or new party programmes in a way that the British Labour Party rarely does, although the recent consultation document on black sections was a move in this direction.

The system is known as *remiss*, the word used by the National Executive at the Labour Party conference when it asks for the *remission* of a motion. In Britain it is remitted to the National Executive but in Sweden *remiss* is a system that takes a policy debate right down to the grass roots of the party. Each member is given a booklet which explains an issue, sets out the policy options and leaves space for members to fill in their views.

Local parties usually organise special meetings where members discuss the issue and try to arrive at a common response which is then filled out on one of the questionnaires and sent in to the party headquarters, where it is fed into the policy making process. The great advantage is that it encourages every member to feel he or she has a role to play and a contribution to make even if they find it difficult to make speeches or articulate ideas.

This system can involve a great many members. Before the 1984 congress, where the party adopted a new programme of ideas, 130,000 copies of the *remiss* booklet were bought by local parties and 1,300 sent in their replies.

The final decision is made by the congress but at the end of such a long policy making process, there is little room for the kind of upsets that can occur at Labour Party conferences in Britain. This can happen at the conference of SSU or the Swedish Labour Women, who attracted a certain amount of ridicule from the party leaders at their 1983 conference when they debated a proposal for erotic-free zones at work. But polices adopted at the three-yearly party congresses are always very carefully thought out and prepared in advance and the disagreements are muted.

The Labour Party would not be keen to adopt the same structure as the SAP for its conference. One only has to imagine what would happen at a Labour Party conference if all the delegates were constituency Labour Party delegates elected by their regional conferences and able to determine the party programme and elect the executive without any separate trade union representation.

Yet it is with a structure of this kind that the SAP has succeeded in developing policies that have won the support of the voters time after time. They have not done so by riding roughshod over the views of party members or by relying on trade unions to deliver bloc votes or by ignoring the policies agreed at their congress. On the contrary they have done it by involving their party membership so deeply in the policy making process, by helping them to acquire the knowledge they need to come to grips with the issues in their study circles, by consulting their rank and file members in a way that does not favour only the active and the articulate and by building up a membership that is far larger and therefore inevitably far more representative of its voters, so that the party has succeeded in harnessing the imagination and intelligence of its membership to the task of policy making.

Members of the SAP are not made to feel that it is just an organisational workhorse that is taken out of the stable at election time. It is a democratic, policy-making body whose main asset is the political education and commitment of its members. As its general secretary Bo Toresson said at the 1984 congress, the SAP preaches democracy to others so it must practice it.

"Our party must serve as a model for the society we wish to create. We talk about local democracy and involving people at grass roots level in the decision-making process. Our party organisation must reflect this process and serve as an example. Every member must be able to say 'I can influence policies in my branch and politics in my local area'."

7. Press and Broadcasting

The British labour movement sat back and watched the death of its only two committed supporters in the national press, the Daily Herald (1964) and the Sunday Citizen (1967), owned by the trade union and the Co-operative movements respectively. It felt unable to do anything, even though a Labour government was elected in 1964.

The Swedish labour movement was not afflicted by the same paralysis when its own newspapers were threatened with a wave of closures in the late 'sixties. The Labour government introduced legislation to give financial support to the smaller newspaper in each circulation area. The Act came into force in 1971.

State support

This selective support was in addition to general subsidies to the press, such as exemption from VAT and subsidies for joint newspaper distribution, and it was paid to those newspapers that reached less than 50 per cent of the households in their circulation areas. Thus in the province of Värmland the main morning newspaper Nya Wermlands Tidning (Conservative) reaches 65 per cent of households and receives no selective support. Its rival Värmlands Folkblad (Labour) reaches 28 per cent of households and received state support to cover 16 per cent of its production costs in 1983.

The theory is that the larger paper in an area should always be able to make a profit but a smaller competitor will have an unequal struggle, as the lion's share of the advertising revenue and all of the economies of scale will go to the larger paper. The state support will not save a bad newspaper from going to the wall, but it will compensate a small newspaper for the unfair advantages of its larger competitor and halt the trend towards local press monopolies.

This has worked. In Britain, as the table shows, the number of towns or cities with competing evening newspapers has sunk from 24 after the first world war to only two in 1973 and now none since the closure of the Glasgow Evening Citizen (1974) and the merger of the London Evening News (1980). In Sweden there were 50 communities with competing daily newspapers which dropped to 20 by the early 'seventies. And now, thanks to state support, 19 of those areas still have competing papers.

In Sweden the government acted in time to preserve a choice of newspapers in most of the cities which is particularly important in a country that has no genuinely national newspapers because overnight distribution is prohibitively expensive over such distances. At the same time the Labour government preserved its most precious asset, the Labour press, which would otherwise have perished as surely as it did in this country.

The Swedish Conservatives and the Swedish Newspaper Publishers' Association, while in favour of general subsidies to the press, were bitterly against selective support. It was an infringement of the freedom of the press, it was an attack on free enterprise, it would disrupt the functioning of the market, they said. But now they have had to change their minds. The biggest Conservative newspaper in Sweden, Svenska Dagbladet, has happily accepted the maximum subsidy for a number of years, receiving 39 million kronor (about £3½ million) in 1984. The Centre Party, with relatively few newspapers, has also benefited from the support and has been able to launch a number of new weekly papers. But the main beneficiary of state support has undoubtedly been the SAP.

It is not that the state support has guaranteed their papers against closure. A bold attempt to relaunch their morning newspaper in the Stockholm area, *Stockholms Tidningen* was forced into bankruptcy in 1984 when the labour movement refused to advance any more money. But the labour movement has been so determined to hang on to its established newspapers, giving them subsidies from their own money to tide them over difficult periods, lending them money to invest in modern plant, that none of them has folded. In 1971 there were 21 Labour daily newspapers. Today there are 21. The party has even been able to launch some new weekly newspapers.

The result is that in most towns and cities in Sweden there is a Labour newspaper circulating. In some of the northern towns the Labour paper is the biggest and therefore receives no subsidy. In Pitea the Labour *Pitea-Tidning* reaches 82 per cent of households. In Solleftea the Labour *Nya Norrland* reaches 70 per cent. But almost everywhere else in the country it is the smaller paper competing against a Conservative or Liberal rival.

On the island of Gotland there is a unique system where the Labour Party shares a newspaper with the Centre and Liberal parties. The paper always carries the same advertisements, but the editorial content varies between the *Gotland People's Paper* (Labour) and the *Gotlander* (Centre-Liberal) and as a result they both qualify for a special government collaboration grant. Without the scheme the *Gotlands Allehanda* (Conservative) would have a monopoly.

The existence of the Labour press, although it accounts for only 20 per cent of the newspapers sold in Sweden, makes an enormous difference to the labour movement. For one thing it gives the Labour Party a voice (or rather 21 voices) in public debate. This moves the perception of 'public opinion' and 'the consensus' several notches to the left. It also gives each issue in public debate a firm anchor on the left so that the floating voters do not just drift into a right-wing view because that is the only one that has been expressed.

It also ensures that the party's views cannot be misrepresented or, even worse, ignored by the press or radio or television. In Britain Labour politicians are all too familiar with the point that always seems to be played down or never gets picked up in the papers and, since television and radio take their news 'values' from the papers, it never gets picked up there either. In Sweden the same stories cannot be ignored if they figure prominently in the 21 papers of the A-press, the Labour press.

Equally the A-press can play up or pick up stories that the bourgeois press would prefer to ignore. The fall of the Centre-Liberal-Conservative coalition under the Centre Party leader Thorbjörn Fälldin in 1978 was largely the work of the A-press papers which drove Falldin to resign by publishing details of the bitter quarrels between the parties within the coalition government. "The other newspapers didn't seem to have the will or the energy to cover the story," said Rolf Alsing of the Labour newspaper Värmlands Folkblad.

It is undoubtedly true that the existence of strong Labour newspapers in some parts of Sweden strengthens the Labour vote, though it is as difficult to prove this as it is to prove that the existence of an overwhelmingly hostile Tory press harms the Labour Party in Britain. "There is a certain correlation between the strength of the SAP and a strong Labour press in certain areas, but you don't know which came first, the chicken or the egg," said Rolf Alsing. "All you can say is that there is a strong Labour vote in Malmo, where there is the biggest Labour morning newspaper in the country, *Arbetet*, while the Labour vote has traditionally been weak in Gothenburg where there is no Labour newspaper."

An agenda of debate

The existence of a Labour paper certainly has an effect on other newspapers in the same area. For one thing the competition makes the other newspapers significantly better. But it also means that the bourgeois press does not attack Labour quite so freely or carelessly, when it knows Labour can hit back. It sets limits on their actions.

But the main effect of a Labour press is that the Labour Party can set an agenda of debate. It can make people discuss the issues that it wants to see discussed and does not have to fight all its battles on the other parties territory. It has the effect of shifting the entire political spectrum to the left. It not only means that people are more ready to vote Labour, but that the Liberal and Central parties are further to the left. This was shown most graphically during the Vietnam war when all the main parties in Sweden, including Centre, Liberal and even Conservatives, joined in criticism of the American conduct of the war.

The British Labour Party, on the other hand, has no daily newspapers of its own. Nor have the trade unions, though they have spent a long time talking about it. Labour does receive support from the Mirror Group at election time and, sometimes, in a more ambiguous way, from the Guardian. But there is all the difference in the world between a newspaper that argues a case constantly and persuasively as the A-press argues for the labour movement in Sweden, and newspapers that sometimes argue for some of the policies of the Labour but might switch to the SDP two days before polling day. More important is the fact that no regional or local daily or weekly newspaper in England or Wales supports Labour and only one in Scotland (the West Highland Free Press).

It is not in the British tradition for newspapers to tie themselves too firmly to any political party and that is healthy for the newspapers. But it is not healthy for the Labour Party to fight elections with two rather undependable allies and seven sworn enemies. Its only safe course is to have newspapers of its own.

The Swedish Labour Party never tires of complaining that they have only 20 per cent of the Swedish press and the bourgeois press have 80 per cent and that there are 40 Swedish towns where there is no Labour newspaper at all. They are right to complain. No country is ever fully democratic until it has a balanced as well as a free press. And the democratic socialist case – that socialism can only be achieved by democratic means – is always flawed when Labour parties have to fight with the handicap of a hostile press. But if the British Labour Party had half the Labour press that Sweden has it would be well pleased.

The rise of the British local newspaper monopoly

	1921	1948	1973
Towns with competing evening newspapers	24	12	2
Towns with monopoly evening newspapers	38	55	77

8. The Labour Movement

So far we have looked at only a few of the arms of the labour movement in Sweden, the A-press, which owns the Labour newspapers, the ABF, which organises the study circles, the youth section SSU and the SAP itself, but none of these can give an adequate explanation of the extraordinary durability of the Swedish Labour Party's vote at a time when the British Labour Party's vote appears to be in a spiral of decline.

To gain a better understanding we have to stand back and look at the whole breadth of the Swedish labour movement which is a far bigger family of organisations than it is in Britain and covers a far wider range of activities and age groups.

To begin at the beginning, the Young Eagles are the labour movement's answer to the Scouts. They were formed in 1931 "in order to counteract the Scout movement and certain religious organisations with rather authoritarian ideals" and they make no secret of the fact that their aim is "to impress the values of the labour movement on new generations."

Their current membership is 70,000 and in addition they organise after-school activities for another 30,000 children. In Sundbyberg, for instance, while the SAP employed an agent and a clerical worker and the SSU had an agent on temporary assignment, the Young Eagles had ten fulltime employees running their latchkey clubs in the town on grants from the local authority. Their only British equivalent is the Woodcraft Folk.

The SSU is already familiar to readers but there are several other sections in the Swedish Labour Party, the SSKF, the women's organisation, which has some 50,000 members, the Brotherhood movement, based on the Christian Socialists in Britain but a good deal larger with 9,000 members, and Verdandi, the party's own temperance movement, which believes that an active life is the answer to alcoholism. It organises outdoor activities for its 50,000 members, but it does not insist on total abstinence.

The Co-operative movement was also based on the British model but has grown into a giant in the Swedish economy taking nearly 25 per cent of the retail trade in consumer foods and owning most of the country's supermarkets and hypermarkets. There is an oil co-op, OK, with 15 per cent of petrol sales and a co-operative insurance company which is Sweden's biggest insurer. The Co-op Union also publishes two of Sweden's biggest magazines with circulations of 500,000 and 350,000.

Activities

The Swedish labour movement differs not only in scale but in scope, reaching into activities that are quite unknown in the British labour movement such as entertainments, parks, zoos and sports clubs which have their origin in the earliest days of the workers' struggle.

As the official history of the Swedish labour movement relates: "To begin with the workers did not have anywhere to hold their meetings. The employers and the bourgeois establishment would not hire their assembly halls to them. They were often forced to hold their meetings by the roadside and in parks. The workers decided to get their own places where they could have their meetings. In 1891 the first People's Hall was opened in Kristianstad and in 1893 the first People's Park was inaugurated in Malmo.

"With great sacrifices and great idealism People's Halls and People's Parks were set up all over the country and from the very start they were not just places to meet. It was just as important to raise funds for political work by arranging events, such as parties, dances, theatre and entertainment."

Today there are 650 People's Halls and 160 People's Parks which are owned by the labour movement but their activities are largely subsidised by the state and the local authorities. Many of the parks include zoos and the halls provide most of the dances and live entertainment in the country with their central organisation acting as the leading agency for orchestra, theatre and film. They also help local SAP branches to build up a cultural side to their activities. The party has set itself the target that every branch should be able to provide some form of entertainment, such as a choir or a revue group, with their street meetings by the end of the decade.

Quite apart from the Co-op Union, which has its own manufacturing group, KF Industry, there are a number of other important co-operatives. There is a housing co-operative, HSB, which is one of the main providers of low cost housing with some 250,000 dwellings owned and managed by their tenant-owners.

There are two building companies owned by trade unions the BPA, which grew out of building guilds set up by the building trade unions in the 'twenties on the model of British guild socialism and is now one of the largest building companies in Sweden, and *Riksbyggen*, set up by the building trade unions in the thirties to create jobs for their members and now a co-operative housing company. Each builds about 10 per cent of all new houses in Sweden.

Beyond the labour movement there are the "popular movements" which are not strictly a part of it, but many of them have grown out of the labour movement, have been built up by members of the labour movement and are suffused with its ideals. The national tenants' union, HRF, with its 600,000 members, is closely linked to the labour movement. The association of works' sports clubs, *Rikskorpen*, grew out

of the labour movement although its 20,000 member clubs now cover every area of Swedish life.

Most important of all is the pensioners' 'trade union', PRO, which was set up in 1941 but has grown very rapidly to its present membership of 400,000 and has become a very effective lobbyist for the retired. It has no formal links with the SAP but no one can be in any doubt that it springs from the labour movement and helps to draw elderly people into 'the family of labour'.

That is no bad thing because the labour movement gives people a feeling of belonging and being cared for that is often missing in the welfare state. In Sweden people can live their lives in the warm bosom of the labour movement, reading a Labour paper, shopping at the Co-op, taking evening classes at the ABF, going to a dance at the People's Hall, joining in the social activities of their trade union or the SAP branch, leaving the children at the Young Eagles while they go to their study circle. They can completely envelop themselves in the environment of the movement.

Rolling back the state

This may well be part of the explanation for the loyalty and solidarity of the Labour vote in Sweden. Many people now feel, paradoxically, that although the labour movement believed in its early days that everything should be run by the state, indeed that was an essential part of the socialism they were fighting for, it would be better now if some areas taken over by the state were handed back to the labour movement.

"During the period of great reforms in which the state was given ever-increasing responsibilities and ever-greater resources, it was considered natural and correct to let the state take over much of what had previously been done by the labour and popular movements – from libraries to health insurance," says Lars Engqvist, editor of the largest Labour morning newspaper *Arbetet*.

"Something of the original values was lost in the process. But not forever. We realise now that we must establish some sort of balance between the tasks that can really only be performed by the state, the 'strong society', and the activity and personal commitment that finds its expression in the popular movements."

In his view the greatest achievement of the labour and popular movements that grew up at the end of the last century was not just in fighting injustice, but in their members' educating themselves and widening their own horizons. "In their organisations people could try new forms of community, they had a chance to experience a new social pattern. Even in organisations that were not socialist, their activities offered an opportunity to live socialism as a way of life."

Now people are coming to the conclusion that it is better to travel hopefully than to arrive, because the labour movement, although it was created merely as a vehicle for achieving socialism, is itself far more socialist than the society it has brought into being. Was it a socialist advance, for instance, for the ABF, which was one of the pioneers of the library movement in Sweden, to hand over its libraries to the state? Would it be an advance for the ABF, now the biggest provider of adult education in Sweden, to hand over this responsibility to the local authorities?

Of course the ABF is not the only provider of adult education. The other parties have their own associations, the Citizens' School which is run by the Tories and the Adult School, run by the Liberal and Centre Parties, though they are much smaller. There is now another provider on the scene, Komvux, which is backed by the local authorities and offers a purely municipal form of adult education. It also offers an ideological dilemma for the labour movement which it seems likely to resolve firmly in favour of ABF.

The British labour movement has never had the luxury of such dilemmas since it has long ago disbanded or abandoned all arms of the labour movement that were not purely political or industrial. The last time when there was any overlap was when the National Health Service and the National Assistance Board were created and took over some of the functions that had been carried out by trade unions for their members.

But when students of the British labour movement delve a little further back in its history to the heyday of the Clarion cycling clubs, the rambling clubs, the sports clubs that grew around the old Labour League of Youth, the Daily Herald and the Daily Citizen and the Labour newspapers that sprang up before the First World War, the social traditions of the Labour Party, the loyalty of the Co-operative movement in its earlier days, they must wonder whether we have not lost something that is more important than it seemed at the time.

9. Trade Union Links

Speakers at the Trades Union Congress and the Labour Party Conference like to emphasise the strong links between their two organisations, usually in ringing rhetorical phrases such as "We are the indissoluble brotherhood of the Labour Party and the trade unions" or "We are two arms of the same movement, bound together by hoops of steel". And even in their less florid moments the members of both organisations believe, with some pride, that the links between the Labour Party and the trade unions are stronger in Britain than in any other country in the world.

But this is just the labour movement's equivalent of the views that "our police are wonderful" or "our police are the best in the world". It is not based on anything objective and if one looks at the links between the two arms of the labour movement, the most that can be said is that they are strong in parts.

Neil Kinnock and Norman Willis are probably the first leader of the Labour Party and general secretary of the TUC who happen to be firm friends, but relations between the party and the unions at that level have always been close. The same goes for general secretaries of trade unions, members of the national executive committee and Labour ministers or shadow ministers.

But farther down the structure, the shallowness of the relationship begins to show. It has been a rule in the Labour Party since 1962 that trade unionists who want to take part in their constituency Labour Party or want to attend Labour Party conferences, even as delegates of their own union, have to join the Labour Party as individual members (£8 per year) as well as being trade union members (60p a year).

The result is that the link that a constituency Labour Party has with its local trade unions is precisely with those trade unionists who are committed to the Labour Party and sufficiently interested in its affairs to pay the individual subscription as well as the trade union affiliation.

They are often people who are more active in the Labour Party than in their trade union.

It does not normally have any links with the other members of the trade union branches who are not individual members. If it tries it will find it difficult to discover which members of a union branch pay the political levy and which do not, which ones are therefore trade union members of the Labour Party and which are not. It can even be difficult to find out how many of the members live in the constituency, who they are or where they live. It cannot contact them individually.

It would be difficult to exaggerate the difference that this makes in practice. It means that the link, which is so strong at the national level, can be very weak on the ground. And it is often a one-way link. The trade unionists who want to take part in the Labour Party can do so, but the Labour Party finds it very difficult to use the branches of the local trade unions as a means of reaching ordinary trade union members and persuading them to vote Labour.

Two-way relationship

In Sweden, on the other hand, the trade unions have far less influence over the party at national level. They have no bloc votes at the party congress, no reserved places on the party executive, no votes in the election of leader, in fact no privileges at all. But the relationship between the party and the unions is much, much closer. And it is a two-way relationship. The party is the political arm of the trade unions. And the unions are the electoral arm of the party.

The difference is partly a product of history. In Britain the TUC was set up in 1868 and it was the larger unions in the TUC that called the conference that set up the Labour Party in 1900. In Sweden it was the other way round. The Swedish Labour Party was set up first, in 1889, and it was on the initiative of the Swedish Labour Party that the Swedish TUC – the LO – was set up in 1898.

That difference can still be clearly seen in their relationships. The Labour Party was set up to represent the unions in Parliament and in its constitution the unions are still very much the senior partners, able to control the conference and the executive if they wish to. The SAP was set up to represent the workers in parliament and its constitution gives the power to the trade unionist rather than the trade union.

It is the system of trade union affiliation that is vitally different. In the British Labour Party trade unions affiliate at national, regional and local level, but it is the national affiliation that must come first. That gives them the votes at conference. And, although there are complications over the political levy and the election of delegates, a trade union usually casts its votes at Labour Party conference according to its national policy.

In the Swedish Labour Party it is the trade union branch that affiliates to the *arbetarekommun* at local level and all members of the branch then become members of the *arbetarekommun* unless they sign letters of reservation, which are the same as 'contracting out' in Britain. In rare cases, the *arbetarekommun* is a delegate body, but in most areas all members can attend and vote at meetings so trade union members, although they make up the majority in every *arbetarekommun*, vote as individuals and not according to the policy of their trade union.

There has been a long and bitter debate over the issue of affiliation and 'contracting out', with the Conservatives making exactly the same claim as they have in Britain that trade unions make it difficult for members to contract out and with the trade unions rejecting the claim just as emphatically. But the idea of collective affiliation to a political party has become so unpopular (even 65 per cent of LO members are against it) that the SAP has now begun to discuss an alternative form of 'organisational affiliation'.

Political fund ballots

The issues raised by the political fund ballots in Britain are already familiar in Sweden. Many trade union branches have to vote repeatedly on the issue of affiliation. Trade union elections are generally run on party political lines and some union branches change hands frequently between the SAP and the VPK. The Communists invariably call for a vote to disaffiliate from the SAP and the SAP then has to fight to regain control of the branch and reaffiliate. This challenge from the VPK ensures tht the party works hard to keep control of the unions from the bottom up. In the white-collar unions it has similar battles with the Liberals and Conservatives.

For the SAP the importance of winning the battle for affiliation in each trade union branch is not so much financial, as state aid now provides the bulk of their income, but because of the overriding political importance of retaining the support of the most important Labour voter, the industrial worker.

In the run-up to the 1973 election they involved 80,000 of their trade union members in a consultation programme to find out how they felt the law should be strengthened on unfair dismissal, health and safety, worker directors, access to company information and shop stewards' rights. The results were put into the manifesto.

This strategy had several advantages. It enabled to SAP to get out into its affiliated trade union branches and the party's own workplace branches, of which there are 500, and take politics to the workplace. It gave trade union members a tangible benefit for their affiliation. It also gave them an immediate interest in a Labour victory.

They have continued this strategy of taking politics to the trade unionist and have been rewarded by a very high level of political commitment to the SAP in many trade union branches. In the 1982 election, for instance, the metal workers' union was able to involve 14,695 of its members in weekend schools and study circles as part of their £1 million campaign in support of the Labour Party.

LO is also very closely involved in the Labour Party's election campaign and it runs what it calls 'information drives', in other words poster campaigns, urging all its members to support the SAP. It is able to do this because nearly all its member unions are blue-collar and more than half of them are committed in their constitutions to the promotion of a socialist society. The great disadvantage of the TUC is that less than half its member unions are affiliated to the Labour Party, so it has to keep at arm's length from the party, especially at election time. The success of the SAP in retaining the support of trade unionists can be gauged from a poll of the 1979 election which showed that 71 per cent of industrial workers had voted Labour. A similar poll by BBC-Gallup in the British general election of 1983 showed that 39 per cent of trade unionists had voted Labour. The two figures are not statistically comparable, but they are indicative of the huge difference in the degree of loyalty of working class voters to the Labour Party in the two countries. Industrial workers are the backbone of the SAP's support in the way that they once were of Labour's and the SAP feel threatened by de-industrialisation which is so evident in Thatcher's Britain. Their greatest hope now is the re-industrialisation of Sweden that will help to secure their future for a generation ahead.

10. Wage-Earner Funds

The SAP does not expect to win the loyal support of the industrial workers and give nothing in return. On the contrary it has gone out of its way, as we have seen, to find out what reforms the industrial workers would like carried out by a Labour government. It is as a result of this process that the SAP became committed to the idea of wage-earner funds.

It came originally from the LO's chief economist in the early 'seventies, Rudolf Meidner, a bluff German-born Swede, who had been associated with a rather right-wing LO establishment in the 'fifties and 'sixties but was finding that the logic of his own policies was pushing him further to the left.

His idea arose in response to the problem of excess profits in some companies which were a side-effect of the LO's solidarity policy. This was designed to reduce differentials between workers as a step towards equality by giving a lower percentage rise to the higher-paid workers in the annual wage bargain with the employers. It meant, however, that companies employing high-paid workers, such as Volvo, got away with lower pay rises and therefore made higher profits. The problem was how to persuade Volvo workers to accept low pay rises when the company made high profits.

Objectives

Meidner hit on the idea of a tax that would cream away the excess profits and use them to buy shares in the company that would be vested, collectively, in the workers. The Volvo workers would then be rewarded for their self-restraint in the pay round with shares in their company, which they could not sell, but which would bring them voting rights to elect workers to the board, dividends which could be used to train them in management and the chance, eventually, to assume control of their own company. This would achieve four of the Labour movements' objectives at the same time: it would advance equality and industrial democracy, reduce capital accumulation and redistribute wealth.

Meidner published a table to show how his scheme could give workers enough shares to take over some of Sweden's most profitable companies in 20, 25, 35 or 75 years according to the level at which the tax was set. The reaction of Swedish industry was one of unrestrained hysteria. The employers' federation launched a campaign of unprecedented ferocity against the funds. They were "pure and unadulterated socialism". They would lead to a flight of capital and an investment strike, they warned. They were "expropriations". They would mean the "gradual socialisation" of Sweden. On the last point, at least, they were right.

The employers poured millions of kronor into the anti-funds campaign. They financed a huge anti-Labour campaign, even though the SAP had not yet at that stage taken a position on the scheme. This was undoubtedly a part of the reason for Labour's defeat in 1976 after 44 years in office.

Some would say that Marx had foreseen this a century before when he said that if the "expropriators" were ever "expropriated", they would stop at nothing in their defence of their ownership of capital. The funds, gradualistic as they were, threatened the very heart of the system – the ownership of capital – and the owners of capital were the first to grasp their importance. As one of the leaders of the employers' federation said privately to the government: "This is about power and we will fight you every inch of the way."

Meidner's proposal went to the LO congress in 1976 which accepted it in principle but with some reservations. By this time it had a good deal of momentum and when it came before the SAP's triennial congress in 1978 they had little choice but to accept it in principle and with good grace. It was not that the funds had no supporters in the SAP. On the contrary they had many passionate supporters. It was just that the SAP could see the daunting political difficulties of making them an election winner.

In the 1979 election funds were again an issue, even though the SAP was not committed to them and had no proposals to put before the voters. Again the propaganda against the funds contributed to Labour's defeat. It was not until its 1981 congress that the SAP finally adopted a firm proposal. But by then it was very different from the proposal that Meidner had made in 1976.

Instead of the pure form of worker ownership in the original scheme, what was now proposed was that the excess profits tax should be paid into a regional fund belonging to all the workers in the region and it should then be invested in companies, not necessarily the ones paying the tax.

The funds would be controlled by regional boards that would be initially appointed by the government, but ultimately elected. The majority of board members would have to be employee representatives, whether appointed or elected, so the wage-earners would always be in control of the funds. However, one feature remained unchanged from the Meidner plan. Whenever the board bought shares in a company, the workforce in that company would be entitled to have half the voting rights, if they wanted them, up to a ceiling of 20 per cent.

The build-up of the funds would be deliberately slow with about £200 million coming in every year, less than 1 per cent of the value of all quoted shares but even this snail's pace socialism was enough to enable the employers to conjure up a picture in which individual companies could be taken over quite rapidly by trade union bureaucrats who would have no idea how to run them.

Compromises

As the SAP approached the 1982 election it was clear that wage-earner funds were not going to be an election winner. Their concern was to make sure that they were not an election loser. So Olof Palme announced three clear limitations on the operation of the proposed funds in order to answer the fear that the scheme was open-ended: the funds would only collect money until 1990; the maximum that the funds would be allowed to hold in any one company would be 40 per cent; they would be expected yield a real return of 3 per cent on their investments.

This killed off the bourgeois parties' scare campaign and brought the focus of the election back to the issue which helped the SAP to win. Poll analysis has now shown that wage-earner funds were no longer a central issue by the end of the campaign and the SAP is keen to keep it

that way. The funds came into existence formally on January 1 1984, the chairmen and members of the boards were appointed by the autumn and they set to work on the stock market without any signs of the flight of capital or the investment strike that the employers had warned of.

On the contrary Sweden has been experiencing an investment boom with an increase of 15 per cent in industrial investment in 1984. This may not owe much to wage-earner funds whose influence can only have been marginal, but it helps to corroborate the SAP's argument that the funds were a necessary form of public investment to make up for the inadequate investment record of private industry.

The SAP has not sought to convince the public of the need for the funds on ideological grounds but has always based its argument firmly on economic necessities. Funds will be used to invest in the new industries that will secure Sweden's future as a hightly advanced economy. They will also cement together Sweden's wage-bargaining system, because they will dissuade workers in highly profitable industries from using their bargaining strength to the full. The funds will also help to reduce the inequalities of wealth and will strike at the very aspect of industry that has made the problem worse – the tendency of companies to finance growth from retained profits and thus concentrate the wealth among the same group of shareholders. Thus they have a role in providing investment funds, in preventing inflation and redistributing wealth.

The funds however have a role in promoting industrial democracy and this gives them a great ideological importance. The SAP has never been keen on state ownership of industry. It is suspicious of the bureaucracy of state monopolies. It has always been looking for non-state forms of social ownership. Wage-earner funds have provided them with a new way forward that promises socialisation without bureaucratisation. The power of the state is used, not to try to manage every factory, but to enable the workers in the company and the wage-earners as a whole to share in and ultimately to own and to manage the means of their own production, essentially a form of co-operative self-management backed by the legislative power of the state.

Criticisms

But they are by no means universally supported even within the SAP. Their critics argue against them on three grounds. First of all, they claim that wage-earner funds are not an idea that has come in response to pressure from the shopfloor, but one that has been dreamt up by academics at LO headquarters who have foisted it on the party. Secondly, they believe they will bring no tangible benefit to the worker and are just a diversion from the more important tasks of building up the public services and achieving a more equal society, a diversion which has already cost the party six years in power. Thirdly, they argue that the funds have been pushed through too soon before they had been fully tried and tested.

Nevertheless the funds now have a democratic seal of approval since they were a part of the SAP's 1982 manifesto. Since the election the anti-fund campaigners have taken a leaf out of Labour's book and staged a huge demonstration of 100,000 businessmen and business supporters in the centre of Stockholm. After that they set up an 'October 4th Committee' to repeat the demonstration every year. The three bourgeois parties gave a

pledge to abolish the funds if elected and they set up a pre-election Funds Abolition Committee. They produced their own 'Abolish the Funds' car stickers and badges.

All this has created huge waves in the small pool of Swedish policies and has brought confrontation on a scale that seems quite unSwedish. Indeed many of the funds' critics within the party say they must have been imported from the British Labour Party – no other party would put forward a policy that was so unpopular. There has always been a majority against them in the opinion polls. But the SAP has no intention of abandoning its commitment to the funds. It hopes that the voters will come to accept them, now that they can see them in operation, and that the scare campaign will lose plausibility. Gradually the voters will come to see the benefits that the funds bring. If the SAP wins the 1985 election, then by the time of the next election in 1988, the present scheme will nearly have run its course and will, they hope, be as entrenched in the fabric of Swedish society as the health service or the nursery school.

Democratic socialists in other countries can only look on in hope. If any form of social ownership is going to win the support of the electorate for any sustained period, it will not be bureaucratic state ownership. It may be a scheme like wage-earner funds if it leads to a real democratisation of industry. And if any party can achieve this, it is the SAP. It may take them 50 years to do it, but if they don't get there, who will?

11. A Philosophy of Power

In Aesop's Fable the hare runs for a short while and then takes a long rest. The tortoise walks at a steady pace but arrives first. The natural instincts of most members of the British Labour Party would be those of the hare. If they win an election, they want the government to go hell for leather for five years to push through as much of their programme as they can, in case they are defeated at the next election and find themselves out in the political wilderness again.

The Swedish Labour Party's instincts are those of the tortoise. They prefer to stay in power, even if it means taking reform more slowly and advancing at the electorate's pace. They do not believe in rushing reform when the public is not ready for it, because that will only create the conditions for their own defeat. On the other hand they do not sit back and wait for public opinion to catch up with them. They begin a public debate and they try to win the argument.

They are not in the least put out if they are compared with Aesop's tortoise. In fact Olof Palme sometimes makes the comparison himself. And why not? After all, the tortoise arrived first. And the SAP is already a good deal further along the road than any other democratic socialist party.

It would depend on the definition, of course. If socialism were to be defined solely in terms of state ownership of industry, then the SAP could not be said to have advanced any further than many other parties. But that would be a narrow, sectarian definition. Socialism springs from many sources, Marxist, co-operative, libertarian, syndicalist, Christian, and it embraces all forms of social ownership as well as other goals, such as equality and democracy. Progress must be judged against all yardsticks.

Social ownership

And it is important to understand why it has not gone any further down the road of state ownership. One reason is ideological. The SAP fears the bureaucracy of state monopolies. Another reason is electoral. Voters do not like state monopolies either. They will not vote for a party that would create more of them. The SAP is sometimes asked why, if it has been in office for 50 years, it has not nationalised the entire economy. The answer is that it has been in office for 50 years largely because it has not tried to nationalise the entire economy. It has looked instead for more responsive, less bureaucratic, more popular forms of social ownership.

It has also, as we saw in Chapter 2, concentrated on building up the public sector as a whole which is now the largest in the democratic world at 65.4 per cent of gross national product. That represents a high level of public services and a high degree of income redistribution that can only be maintained by a relatively high level of taxation which, in turn, can only be guaranteed by a Labour government. That is why Labour's first priority must be to stay in power. The achievement of this system depended on having long sustained periods of Labour government, not short bursts of radicalism followed by years of

30

opposition, and its continuation now depends equally on having Labour in power.

This is why the SAP has a totally different philosophy of power from the British Labour Party. In Britain the only philosophy of power, if one can call it that, is to win the next election. But the SAP does not simply try to win the next election. It tries to win the election after that. The 1985 election is fought with one eye on 1988.

This is also why the SAP does not try to rush reforms. It is only if a party expects to lose the next election that there is any point in rushing them through. If it works on the expectation that it will win, it can devote more time to consultation and debate. These expectations are often self-fulfilling.

Popular support

The SAP operates on the principle that every reform, if it is to remain secure, needs a degree of consensus behind it. Ideally this means that the SAP will win the support or the abstention of one of the other parties in parliament, usually the Centre or Liberal Parties, even if it means a few minor concessions, because this will guarantee that the reform cannot be reversed by a bourgeois government, indeed it guarantees that it cannot become an election issue. Thus the SAP won the support of the Centre Party for press subsidies when they were introduced, because the Centre Party had very few newspapers of its own, and this undermined the attempts of the Liberals and Conservatives to abolish them.

Obviously there are fundamental issues that split the parties on clear left-right lines, such as state pensions in the 'fifties and wage-earner funds today, and on these issues it is impossible to win Centre or Liberal Party support. But that only increases the importance, in the party's view, of winning public support for the policy. Winning the vote in parliament is not enough. They have to win the argument in the country first as far as they can. If necessary they have to make concessions to public opinion, even though they have the votes in parliament, because every reform must be anchored in public support.

But the SAP does have many more levers on public opinion than the British Labour Party. It has the Labour press. It has a more balanced broadcasting system. And it has its own consultation process within the party, which may only reach party members, but in a country where over 20 per cent of adults are members of their local Labour Parties this is a powerful weapon. Their consultation can also reach out into all the blue-collar trade unions. But just as importantly the system of study circles creates a body of party members who are extremely well versed in the arguments and can take the debate into every workplace.

It was Tony Benn who popularised the phrase in Labour's Programme of 1973 which promised "an irreversible shift in the balance of power and wealth in favour of working people and their families". He seemed to assume that a reform only had to be carried out by a radical Labour government and it would become irreversible, like the National Health Service, the state pension scheme or the social security system. It has taken Mrs Thatcher to disabuse us of the notion that anything is irreversible.

The SAP knows that the only way to make their reforms irreversible is to stay in power and the only way to do that is to win the positive support of the voters, not just the negative support of those who think Labour is better than the alternatives, but the positive support of those who really want Labour to be in power. Thus support for the party must be firmly rooted in support for its policies and a degree of consensus in public opinion. That is why the various bourgeois governments who ruled from 1976 to 1982 found it so difficult to get away from the Labour Party's economic and social policies and were forced to continue Labour's policies in many fields.

The SAP did not take easily to opposition either. They simply did not fit in the opposition mould in a way that the British Labour Party, sadly, has come to do and they had only one overriding ambition: to get back in power.

The SAP is a political machine that is designed for power. Its organisation and career structure and promotion ladder all lead to one place: parliament. And it does not have a well-developed sense of left and right. Members are used to asking themselves not so much what they, personally, would like in an ideal world, but what the electorate can be persuaded to support in the real world. These tactical arguments cut across and confuse the left-right policy arguments. There is a left and a right wing in the party, certainly, but they are the wings of the party, not its body. The great majority of party members will refuse to categorise themselves as either left or right. They are just party members. The result is that few debates are seen in purely left-right terms. They are more likely to be debated on their merits. Thus the image that is projected to the public is of a party engaged in serious debate and not in faction-fighting. When there are arguments between the left and right, as there was in 1984 between the left wing economists in LO and the right-wing finance minister, Kjell-Olof Feldt, over the speed at which Labour's economic policies could be implemented, they evoke great interest simply because they are so rare. This one was called the 'War of the Roses' after the party's symbol, the red rose, and extensively covered in the press.

Attitudes

But the most distinctive characteristic of the SAP is its rather 'gentlemanly' attitude to democracy. In the midst of the state pension scheme crisis in the 'fifties, when the parties were deadlocked, the SAP had a chance to win because a Conservative MP was ill. The Prime Minister, Tage Erlander, refused to call a vote until the MP was better. He did not want an undemocratic victory. He was also the Labour Prime Minister who insisted on the constitutional reforms that removed the upper chamber of parliament, even though Labour had a permanent majority there.

This rather fastidious attitude would infuriate socialists in any other country, but no one can deny that it has worked to the advantage of the Swedish Labour Party in the long run. The danger for a party that has been out of power too long, like the British Labour Party, is that it will show its impatience and try to push through reforms that have not been fully argued out, thus losing the sense of mutual trust that it needs to have with the electorate.

The irony is that those who behave like the hare in Aesop's Fable and believe in pushing through as much socialism as they can before they lose the next election are the traitors to their own cause, because this impatience betrays their belief that socialism is not genuinely popular and must be forced down in large doses before the patient has an opportunity to complain. The SAP works on the opposite assumption that there is a natural majority for socialism in the electorate and as long as they can present the right policies, they can tap that support and win a majority of the votes. And that is precisely what they have done in ten of their last sixteen elections.

There have been times in the 'forties and the 'sixties when the British Labour Party has been able to tap this natural support and has become the natural party of government. But now it has persuaded itself that it is the victim of a sociological trend of inevitable decline in its support. If the experience of the SAP does nothing else, it can at least show that all of these trends and inevitabilities are so much bunk. If they can do it, so can the Labour Party.

12. Conclusion

You might think that, as a party that has suffered a disastrous decline in support over the last 20 years, the Labour Party would be keen to study other parties to find out why they have been more successful and to learn from their experience.

But, sadly, the Labour Party seems to suffer from a post-imperialist delusion that it is the oldest or biggest or best labour movement in the world (none of which are true). It does have regular discussions with its sister parties through the Socialist International, of course, but only on international issues: when it comes to practical issues, it begins to lose interest.

Fortunately this chauvinism has not infected everyone and there has been a trickle of visitors from the Labour Party to Sweden. But they all come up against a common problem. The gap between the two parties is now so wide that it is difficult to know where to start. They can see the lessons to be learnt but they do not know how to turn them into practical steps and simple recommendations that could be put into effect by the Labour Party. There have been useful visits by Jim Mortimer as general secretary and Joyce Gould, assistant national agent, leading to a possible pilot project on study circles. But most visitors come back rather dazed by the experience.

This was certainly the case on a Labour Party delegation of which I was a member with Lord Underhill, then the party's national agent, and Harold Sims, its Yorkshire regional organiser. We arrived in Malmo in the middle of an election and were shown round the city by a group of party agents. They told us that the campaign had been launched a couple of weeks before our arrival at a rally in the Malmo Football Stadium.

"Oh yes," we inquired politely, "and how many people came to the rally?" If they had said 350, we should have felt at home. If they had said 3,500, we should have been impressed. But when they said 35,000 we were so flabbergasted that ev-erything seemed quite unreal from that moment on. It was as though we had walked through the looking-glass.

Explanations

The reaction of most visitors is to look for a simple explanation for the differences that avoids the need to do anything. The easiest is to say that there are so many differences between Britain and Sweden, in their policies and their economies as well as their histories and even their national temperaments, that any comparison is invalid.

But this is difficult to argue. A statistical study by two social scientists in the 'seventies came to the conclusion that, geography and population apart, it would be difficult to find two countries that were more similar. The composition of their population, their workforce and their economy were very close. The main differences were in the labour movement itself: the level of unionisation was much higher in Sweden and the loyalty of trade unionists to the Labour Party was much stronger.

Anyone who has visited cities like Gothenburg and Edinburgh or Newcastle and Malmo will know how strikingly similar they are, lying on roughly the same latitude with the same population and many of the same industries. Nowadays their inhabitants even watch the same television programmes and support the same football teams on Match of the Day.

Another simple 'explanation' of the differences that come readily to hand is state aid to political parties. But this cannot possibly 'explain' the success of the party since it was successful long before state aid started. State aid has not been the cause of

Labour's electoral success, but it has been one of the results of it.

Many others take refuge in the notion that the SAP is "only a social democratic party....", a notion that once again betrays the unspoken assumption that socialism is unpopular with the electorate. It's not true, but if it were, it would not make a difference.

None of these 'explanations' does anything to get away from the simple truth that the SAP is a good deal better organised than the Labour Party and its members are better trained, better informed, better educated and better equipped for the task of winning power.

The purpose of this pamphlet is not to provide a guide to action or a ten-point plan to apply the lessons of Sweden to Britain. That is not possible. There are hardly any ideas that can be simply grafted from one party to another. But what is important is that the Labour Party should understand what it is about the SAP that succeeds and why.

The SAP makes no great claims on its own behalf and certainly does not hold itself up as a model for the British Labour Party. On the contrary it acknowledges that the British labour movement has often provided models for the Swedish labour movement from the Rochdale pioneers to the early Christian socialists and the Trades Union Congress. The SAP has learnt a great deal from Britain. The time has now surely come for the lessons of experience to flow in the opposite direction.

Now read...

Labour and a World Society

Denis Healey

FABIAN SOCIETY NO 499

Hugh O'Shaughnessy

TOWARDS A DEMOCRATIC CENTRAL AMERICA

MEXICO
BELIZE
GUATEMALA
HONDURAS
EL SALVADOR
NICARAGUA
COSTA RICA
PANAMA

Available from the Fabian Society

Fabian Essays in Socialist Thought
(Gower, 1984)
ed. Ben Pimlott
paper £8.50
cased £19.50

Recent Fabian Pamphlets

Tracts

482 Betty Vernon	Margaret Cole 1892-1980	£1.50
483 Tom Ellis, Rosaleen Hughes, Phillip Whitehead	Electoral reform	£1.50
484 Christopher Harvie	Against metropolis	£1.50
485 Bryan Gould, Shaun Stewart, John Mills, Austin Mitchell	Economic recovery: what Labour must do	£1.50
486 Nicholas Kaldor	The economic consequences of Mrs Thatcher	£1.50
487 David Donnison	Urban policies: a new approach	£1.00
488 Emma MacLennan, Chris Pond, Jill Sullivan	Low pay: Labour's response	£1.50
489 Roy Hattersley, Eric Heffer, Neil Kinnock, Peter Shore	Labour's choices	£0.90
490 David Downes	Law and order: theft of an issue	£1.50
491 David Blunkett, Geoff Green	Building from the bottom: the Sheffield experience	£1.50
492 Keith Ewing	The Conservatives, trade unions, and political funding	£1.50
493 G. Bernard Shaw	The Fabian Society: its early history (reprinted with a preface by Melvyn Bragg)	£1.50
494 Raymond Plant	Equality, markets and the State	£1.50
495 Bernard Crick	Socialist values and time	£1.50
496 Anthony Wright, John Stewart, Nicholas Deakin	Socialism and decentralisation	£1.50
497 Carl James	Occupational pensions: the failure of private welfare	£1.50
498 eds. Brian Abel-Smith & Peter Townsend	Social security: the real agenda	£1.50
499 Hugh O'Shaughnessy	Towards a democratic Central America	£1.50
500 Peter Townsend	Why are the many poor?	£1.50
501 Denis Healey	Labour and a world society	£1.50
502 Michael Mann	Socialism can survive: social change and the Labour Party	£1.50

Special Centenary Publication

100 Years of Fabian Socialism	£2.50

Books available from the Fabian Society

Patricia Pugh	Educate, Agitate, Organize – 100 years of Fabian Socialism (Methuen, 1984)	cased £19.50
ed. R.H.S. Crossman	New Fabian Essays (Dent 1970)	cased £1.75
ed. Ben Pimlott	Fabian Essays in Socialist Thought (Gower 1984)	cased £19.50 paper £8.50
ed. Howard Glennerster	The Future of the Welfare State (Heinemann, 1983)	paper £5.95
eds. M. Cannell & N. Citrine	Citrine's ABC of Chairmanship (NCLC, 1982)	paper £3.50
J.P.M. Millar	The Labour College Movement	cased £5.50

Postage: books 50p per title (ABC of Chairmanship 30p), pamphlets postfree.

The Swedish Road To Socialism

Sweden will soon have had a socialist government for 50 years – longer than any other democracy. *Martin Linton* sets out to explain what it is about the Swedish Labour Party that succeeds and why. The pamphlet is not, however, a guide to action or a blueprint for the British Labour Party to follow. He describes the Party's ideology, organisation, policy making process, political education programme and press as well as its links with trade unions and the whole range of organisations that make up the Swedish labour movement. But in order to explain its success fully, it is necessary to go deeper into the Party's approach to electoral politics, the pace of reform, the shaping of public opinion and the need to win not one but successive elections. Unlike the British Labour Party, it has understood that the only way to make a policy irreversible is to remain in power and win the positive support of the electorate. He concludes that the Swedish Labour Party has learnt a great deal from its British counterpart in the past and the time has come for the lessons of experience to flow in the opposite direction.

Fabian Society

The Fabian Society exists to further socialist education and research. Since 1884 it has enrolled thoughtful socialists who wish to discuss the essential questions of democratic socialism and relate them to practical plans for building socialism in a changing world. Beyond this the Society has no collective policy. It is affiliated to the Labour Party. Anyone who is not ineligible for membership of the Labour Party is eligible for full membership; others may become associate members. For membership and publications details, write to: General Secretary, Fabian Society, 11 Dartmouth Street, London SW1H 9BN.

£1.50